Other books by *wu wei*
AVAILABLE WHEREVER BOOKS ARE SOLD
The Zen of Happiness
The I Ching
I Ching Wisdom
I Ching Wisdom, Volume II
A Tale Of The I Ching
I Ching Life
I Ching Readings
The I Ching Workbook
50 Yarrow Stalks From China

The god game

By wu wei

POWER PRESS
Los Angeles, California

wu wei

For information, contact:

    Power Press, 1310 Riviera Ave., Venice, CA 90291
    Telephone: (310) 392-9393 Fax: (310) 392-7710
    Email to wu wei: wuwei@power-press.com
    Website: www.power-press.com

ISBN 0-943015-40-5
Copyright © 2001 Power Press
First Edition
10 9 8 7 6 5 4 3 2

wu wei

For Wilfried and Gisela Eckhardt

wu wei

The god game

wu wei

It was about half past three in the morning, in that quiet time when the world renews itself. I was sitting before the fireplace, watching the flames turn the logs into glowing shapes and strange images. I listened to the crackle and pop of the fire and saw the occasional shower of sparks. The unburned portions of logs created dark caves through which I could see the white hot embers at the heart of the fire. Like many of our ancestors over the ten thousand or so years since fire was first mastered, I stared into the flames, enchanted, seeing fantastic images, letting thoughts come as they would.

wu wei

As I sat there, half wondering, half dreaming, I found myself wondering what it would be like to be God, the popular conception of God: all powerful, all-seeing, and all-knowing. I was startled when my first thought was,

"How boring!

There would be nobody to talk to, at least not on God's level, and what is there to talk about anyway, when everything is known, past, present, and future? There would be nothing to do God hadn't done, nothing to see God hadn't seen, and nothing to know God didn't know. And because, as God, I'd be a permanent fixture, it was horrifying beyond even the wildest, most extravagant thought I could conjure up.

wu wei

The situation I imagined was intolerable, at least to my tiny, human imagination.

I wondered what God would do in such a circumstance. The answer came, fully formed, as if I had swallowed a capsule with the information inside. I knew beyond any doubt, at least in my own mind, what God would do, had done.

God would create a game to play.

wu wei

I could see it as if the game were laid out before me—as indeed it was! If it had come in a box, it would have been labeled,

"The God Game."

What God wanted to do more than anything else was to end the boredom—and not just for a little while, but for a long time—almost eternally. I say *almost* eternally because it *was* a game, and, like all games, needed to have an ending. What God wanted, needed, was to have the fresh, exhilarating experience that comes from *not* knowing what's around the next bend in the road.

God wanted to experience 'experience'.

That's what this game would be about—the experience of experiencing.

wu wei

II

God wanted to experience the ultimate of ultimates: joy, rage, rapture, pain, passion, love, wonder, happiness, degradation, hopelessness, sadness, hate, ecstasy, sickness, health, disgust, bliss, boredom, gratitude, reverence, loathing, longing, envy, disdain, devotion, fear, lust, terror, tenderness, excitement, panic, heartache, satisfaction, defeat, winning, disappointment, anger, desire, delight, exultation, dread, losing, celebration, triumph, failure, horror, kindness, gentleness, affection—and one of the greatest, ego.

wu wei

God wanted to experience God

in all the trillion trillion ways that everything in the Universe experiences everything in the Universe.

Isn't that what we're all doing—experiencing?

We're all God—we couldn't be anything else—there was nothing else to begin with—so, everything that came after God was and is and ever will be, nothing less than God.

wu wei

I began to think about the thought process that might have gone into the creation of the game. Of course, God might have just willed it into being with one mighty thought, but I couldn't do that because, although I'm God, as you are God, I have only a tiny bit of all the original God powers, and I had to think my way through it.

wu wei

I began by thinking what the game would be like, what it would *have* to be like, for Me, as God, to be able play. There were two major problems. The first was my omniscience, my all-knowingness. If I didn't get rid of my ability to see into the future, knowing everything, the game wouldn't be any fun. There would be no suspense, no

waiting-to-see-what-was-coming,

no sense of mystery. Of course, as God, I would have already looked into the future and seen what was coming, so I would have to figure out a way around that most difficult problem.

wu wei

The second problem was that I needed a game board to play on. I solved both problems with one stroke: As God, I created the Universe. Instead of playing *on* the board, I would play *in* the board. Actually, I would *be* the board. The board was made from Myself, and I used up *all* of Myself in creating it. I spread my energy to infinity and to eternity, willing it to create. To create what? Well, look around; that's what I created: All-That-Is.

As God, the greatest deed I ever did was the creation of the Universe. After that, everything became possible, even easy in comparison.

"Universe" is derived from the Latin words," unus" meaning "one," and "versus," meaning, "to turn into." It means "one" "turned into" the Universe. The creators of the early Latin language also conceived of God becoming the Universe. Isn't that interesting?

wu wei

The other major problem, the one about my omniscience, my all-knowingness and all-seeingness, was solved when I turned Myself into all those little bits and pieces of the Universe. My God awareness, God knowledge, God power, and God creativity were spread out over the totality, each little particle receiving its share, and therefore, my all knowingness and all seeingness, which before had been concentrated, and therefore potent, was now spread out over the entirety, and was so reduced in potency that I could only get glimpses of the future and the past.

wu wei

And, wonder of wonders, *every* manifested particle was different from every other manifested particle. Now, *that* is some feat. Talk about diversification, it was/is total!

In the creation of the Universe, I used up all of Me; there was no little box with leftover mountain ranges, skies, galaxies, stars, or planets in it. Everything was used up, and everything was in its exact right place; it still is.

We cannot be out of place in the Universe.

Wherever we are, that's where we're supposed to be, the only place we can be, doing whatever it is we're doing.

wu wei

That, all by itself, should bring each of us a degree of peace, knowing we're in the right place at the right time. Even though by being in that place at that time, we might stub a toe, or worse, we are still in the right place at the right time. Furthermore, whatever is happening to us at that moment is for our best benefit. Nothing else that could possibly happen could benefit us more. That's because of Who-We-Are. I, as God, certainly was not going to create a Universe in which truly bad things could happen to Me because if one truly bad thing could happen to Me, so could two, three, and more, leading to the possibility of total destruction.

Therefore, it is a Law of the Universe that only the very best thing can happen to Us at any moment.

It may seem bad, look bad, feel bad—it may hurt us, take something from us: a prized possession, a loved one, or even a part of ourselves, but in the final outcome—in My Universe—whatever happens will ultimately benefit us—and everything else in the Universe as well.

That's because the entire Universe is
made from Me,
is Me,
and
All *Is* One.

Acting on the basis of that information will bring us great
happiness and vast abundance because

it is what is.

wu wei

Acting on the basis of "what is," always brings about happiness and abundance because all the laws of the Universe are based on "what is." Because each manifested particle has a tiny bit of all of my original God information, each one of us knows, at some level, "what is," but because we get caught up in the game of life, we forget to take time to look inside for the information.

Of course, I couldn't abandon my powers without a set of rules by which the game was to be played because that would leave everything in the hands of blind chance, what today is called, "chaos." If I had done that, and something went wrong, there would just be oblivion, as when the lights go out, and because I was/am eternal, as is My Universe, the lights would be out *forever*.

A word on chaos. Real chaos, meaning utter disorder and confusion, is an impossibility in my Universe. *Only* complete order exists. If *anything* less than complete order could exist, my Universe, meaning Me, would be in danger of destruction because *anything* could happen, including destruction.

That is not a possibility.

This Universe has been in existence for approximately 18 billion years—pristine, exquisite, infinite, and eternal.

The Universe is *exactly* as it should be.

Because I did not want the lights to go out forever, into being came The Laws of the Universe, the rules that would govern the game. As you might imagine, the first law I created was the Law of Conservation of Energy, which provides that *none* of the energy in my newly created Universe could *ever* be lost or damaged, only changed. That's because everything that exists is made from Me, is Me, and I didn't want to lose any of Me.

wu wei

Because, as God, I wanted to keep the game interesting, the next Law was that of Change. That Law provides that everything in the entire Universe will be in a state of constant change and constant motion—everything except the Laws; they will remain unchanging, at least until the game is won.

Please take note that I did not say won or lost.

The possibility of losing is zero—there is only winning. It may take a long time to win, perhaps billions or trillions of years, but the game *will* be won in the end.

On the path to winning, it may sometimes seem as if one or more of us is losing, but that's just because we are not paying attention to the rules of the game, and we've either forgotten Who-We-Are or we haven't taken the time to find out.

Paying attention to the Laws, working in harmony with them, brings great pleasure, supreme happiness, great abundance, and the sure knowledge that everything is just the way it's supposed to be. Not paying attention to the laws brings us pain and unhappiness. Why? Because that's how we realize we're doing something that is off the path to winning.

wu wei

Those unpleasant experiences are showing us we have strayed off the path.

The next law was Cause and Effect. That Law provided for a response to every change or action, with the response being in perfect accord with the change or action. Cause and Effect is a flowing of events—smooth, unbroken, and flawless, one change or action producing another—in perfect harmony— in perfect accord with the Laws of the Universe. Once we learn to master the game, we know what causes produce what effects; in other words, what actions to take that will produce the conditions we desire.

In *every* situation or condition, by taking the appropriate action, we can bring about any other condition or situation of life we choose. Knowing that All-That-Is responds to us as we are being at every moment, we can make changes within ourselves that will produce the outer conditions of life that are nearest and dearest to our hearts. Isn't that nice? Would I, as God, have created it in any other way? Would You?

wu wei

Because of the Law of Cause and Effect, a rock thrown into a pond makes ripples—every time—the bigger the rock, the bigger the ripples. Just as we can depend on that to be true and never be disappointed, we can depend on all the causes to produce the same effects every time.

As God, I made many physical laws, laws that would govern matter, such as the Law of Gravity, a force of attraction that holds celestial bodies in their orbits and that on Earth assures that things fall down and not up.

As God, I created light, one of the greatest wonders of My new Universe, and a law that controls the maximum speed of light. That law provides that light will travel at a velocity of 186,000 miles per second, and no more.

That is 669,600,000 miles per hour.

When a photon of light leaves the sun, which is ninety-three million miles from earth, it takes eight minutes and twenty seconds for it to reach this spectacularly beautiful planet.

wu wei

Each photon of light is a tiny packet of energy. It's energy is not released until the photon comes into contact with an object which causes the packet to explode, releasing its energy. For instance, when we stand in the sun we can feel it's heat because we are being bombarded with trillions of tiny photons that hit us traveling 660,600,000 miles per hour which explode on contact, releasing their energy as heat.

The photons of light that enter our eyes, create color and form.

We have never seen anything other than light.

We have never seen a horse or a cow, our parents or our friends, not even ourselves—all we have ever seen are the light rays that reflected off those objects into our eyes where they formed images that were received in our brains which formed a picture. We have never seen the objects themselves. And the picture is not even "out there." It is *entirely* inside our brains—it only seems as if it's "out there."

When the photons of light coming from the sun enter the earth's atmosphere, some of them collide with molecules or dust particles and scatter, causing the sky to appear blue.

wu wei

It is interesting to note that light is not propelled, as when we throw a ball, but whenever light exists, such as when we strike a match, or turn on a light, or gas burns on a distant star, the photons of light travel at that amazing speed of 660,600,000 miles per hour. Some of the photons of light that we see travel through space for millions of years before they reach our eyes. Therefore, when we look into the night sky, we are actually looking back in time to when those photons were first created. The distant stars that produced those photons may have become extinguished thousands or even millions of years ago.

As God, I created the Law of Evolution. That Law provides for the development of organisms along lines that lead toward ever greater complexity and consciousness. Eventually, after billions of years, roughly about eighteen billion, that Law brought forth Thinking Beings, each one gifted with a tiny portion of all my original God powers: the power to imagine, to do, to create, and to destroy. I do not mean to destroy in the total sense of the word (I left that power out when I created the Law of Conservation of Energy); I mean to destroy in the sense of returning a portion of All-That-Is to its original energy state.

wu wei

When paper burns, for example, it releases itself as heat energy, which is absorbed back into the mass of total energy, or as when someone dies. The physical part of that person remains physical, although it decomposes and changes into another form, but the part of the person that is not physical, the Universal intelligence part, or the spirit or the soul, however we choose to think about it, continues to exist. It may just be reabsorbed into the total energy field, or we may keep our personality, so to speak, but either end is glorious.

We may have forgotten how we came to this planet,
but we surely know the way, and what we've done
once, we can do again.

The greatest honor one can have
is to be part of the Universe.

And who the Universe honors with existence, who
has been deemed worthy to receive air and water and
the substance of the earth, we should not disdain.

wu wei

As God, I wanted us to know when we were on the path to winning and losing, so I created all the variations of pain and joy. Whenever we felt happiness, ecstasy, exhilaration, peace, pleasure, love, wonderment, reverence, thankfulness, joy, or feelings like those, we'd be on the path to winning; when we felt unhappiness, frustration, hopelessness, avarice, hatred, greed, thoughtlessness, anger, revengefulness, ingratitude, pain, or feelings like those, we'd be on the path toward losing. Once we learned to recognize the signs of winning and losing, we could make the necessary adjustments to our thoughts and actions to remain on the path to winning. As God, I made the path to

winning more pleasurable so we would be encouraged to follow it.

To make the path more interesting, I created earthquakes, tornadoes, tidal waves, fierce storms, floods, plagues, viruses, drugs, alcohol, hurricanes, music, flowers, avalanches, sex, spontaneity, war, and peace. I also created one of the greatest, love, and one of the funniest, atheism. That last one means I don't believe in Me.

Because, as God, I had created eternity within which to play,

wu wei

I "rigged the game" which means I tipped the scales toward winning because never to win through all eternity would be the same as losing, and I didn't want to lose.

What does it mean "to tip the scales toward winning?" It means that My Universe is favorably inclined. It means that there is slightly more light force than dark, that the more favorable outcome is favored over the less favorable outcome, that we have a better chance of achieving our goals than not, and it means that everything has a better chance of working out in our favor than not.

Would I, knowing I was creating a game for Myself to play, create it any other way?

wu wei

Would You?

At some point in time, we will all win. In my Universe, We cannot lose. We are indestructible children of a golden Universe. We *are* the Universe, a part of it. We are Me. Remember that, and you will play the game differently, with more confidence, more love, more enthusiasm, more playfulness, with more of a carefree attitude, with more trust, and with more care for your fellow humans. And why not? You are the Universe, you are Me. So are They.

So I would be able to enjoy what I had done to the fullest, I

created the law of Free Will. That law provides for all thinking beings to do exactly as they please without reservation. It is *total* free will, unbounded and without limitation. As God, I wanted to be able to play the game and do *exactly* as I pleased. I wanted to be able to experience anything and everything, which is why I created the game in the first place. Therefore, You, as God, may do exactly as you please; the more inventive you are, the more you push out the boundaries of your experience the better—but remember—the unbreakable, unbending law of Cause and Effect is also part of the game.

It wouldn't be any fun if no one could appreciate what I had done, especially Me, so, the moment you come to know Who-You-Are, You will also know what I have done (what You have done) and I will be able to experience that through you. What a thrill!

When any one of Us finally perceives who He or She is, it is like opening the greatest gift of all time, and finding out we get to keep it forever! It is the greatest experience of this or any lifetime.

It is absolutely one of My favorite experiences.

wu wei

Which brings us to the object of the game, a way to win.
So, what is the object of the game?

For all Thinking Beings to become aware of
Who-They-Are.

Using our free will, and our intellect, and our intuition, and our perception, we finally figure out Who-We-Are. Every single thinking being does not have to figure it out on his or her own. When most of Us have figured out Who-We-Are, a point of critical mass will be achieved at which time Everyone will become aware of Who-They-Are and the game will be won.

Hooray for You, hooray for Me, hooray for Us! That will be a time of such exultation and ecstasy that it will create a climax of joy so great, so intense, as to eclipse even the moment I created the Universe, and instantly all parts of Me will come back together again in the sheer joy of unity, knowing We-Are-All-One.

So, I spread out my entire Being to infinity and to eternity, willing it to create. I had a place to play and rules that governed the game, rules that even I couldn't break, and the game was on, and I could play.

Welcome to the game!

wu wei